GOD MADE
THE WORLD

GOD MADE THE WORLD is part of the "God Made" series produced in collaboration with The Faraday Institute for Science and Religion.

Other titles in the series:

GOD MADE SPACE
GOD MADE ANIMALS

ABOUT THE AUTHORS

Steph Bryant loves animals, exploring, and enjoying nature. She became a wholehearted Christian while studying science at Cambridge University, when she began to realise that the wonder she felt in exploring science was really an invitation to worship God. Steph is passionate about looking after the world God has entrusted us with and, after working in conservation science, chose to spend her time helping young people explore the wonder of God's creation and our responsibility to care for it well.

Lizzie Henderson grew up loving God and exploring His creation through science. She is fascinated by the processes God uses to bring about creation's amazing diversity, and loves to encourage young people to find wonder in exploring what God has made. Since studying science at Cambridge University, Lizzie has been busy developing The Faraday Institute's Youth and Schools Programme, helping thousands of young people to explore their questions about science, faith, and our understanding of the universe.

Steph and Lizzie are the Youth and Schools Programme Co-Directors at The Faraday Institute for Science and Religion.

ABOUT THE PROJECT

The Faraday Institute is an interdisciplinary research and communication enterprise linked to the University of Cambridge. Our Youth and Schools Team are committed to providing high-quality events and resources that encourage young people of all ages and backgrounds to explore their questions about the interactions of science and religious faith in exciting and engaging ways.

If you and your children have enjoyed reading about how "God made the world", why not explore more about science, faith, and what God has made at **www.faradaykids.com.** You'll find activities, videos, age-specific answers to common questions, and more about our other resources. You can also share your experience of reading this book with us! Or check out **www.faradayeducators.com** for information about resources and events for parents, teachers, and other educators.

This project and publication was made possible through the support of a grant from the John Templeton Foundation. The opinions expressed in this publication are those of the authors and do not necessarily reflect the views of the John Templeton Foundation.

Text copyright © 2020 Steph Bryant and Lizzie Henderson

This edition copyright © 2020 Lion Hudson IP Limited

Illustrations by Steph Marshall

The right of Steph Bryant and Lizzie Henderson to be identified as the authors of this work has been asserted by them in accordance with the Copyright, Designs and Patents Act 1988.

Published by
Lion Hudson Limited
Wilkinson House, Jordan Hill Business Park
Banbury Road, Oxford OX2 8DR, England

www.lionhudson.com

ISBN 978 0 7459 7784 3

First edition 2020

Acknowledgments: Scripture quotations taken from the ESV® Bible (The Holy Bible, English Standard Version®), copyright © 2001 by Crossway Bibles, a publishing ministry of Good News Publishers. Used by permission. All rights reserved.

A catalogue record for this book is available from the British Library

Printed and bound in China, October 2019, LH54

GOD MADE THE WORLD

Steph Bryant and Lizzie Henderson
Illustrated by Steph Marshall

LION
CHILDREN'S

God made the world.
  He made everything that has
ever existed in the whole world!

From HUGE
powerful things
to tiny delicate ones.

God has given us lots of clues about HOW He made the world.

This is how we think He did it.

God started making the world a very long time ago, using His AMAZING stars.

Stars sparkle and shine because they are really, really hot, like enormous bonfires.

Inside them, tiny bits called "particles" are squashed and squished together into new, bigger bits.

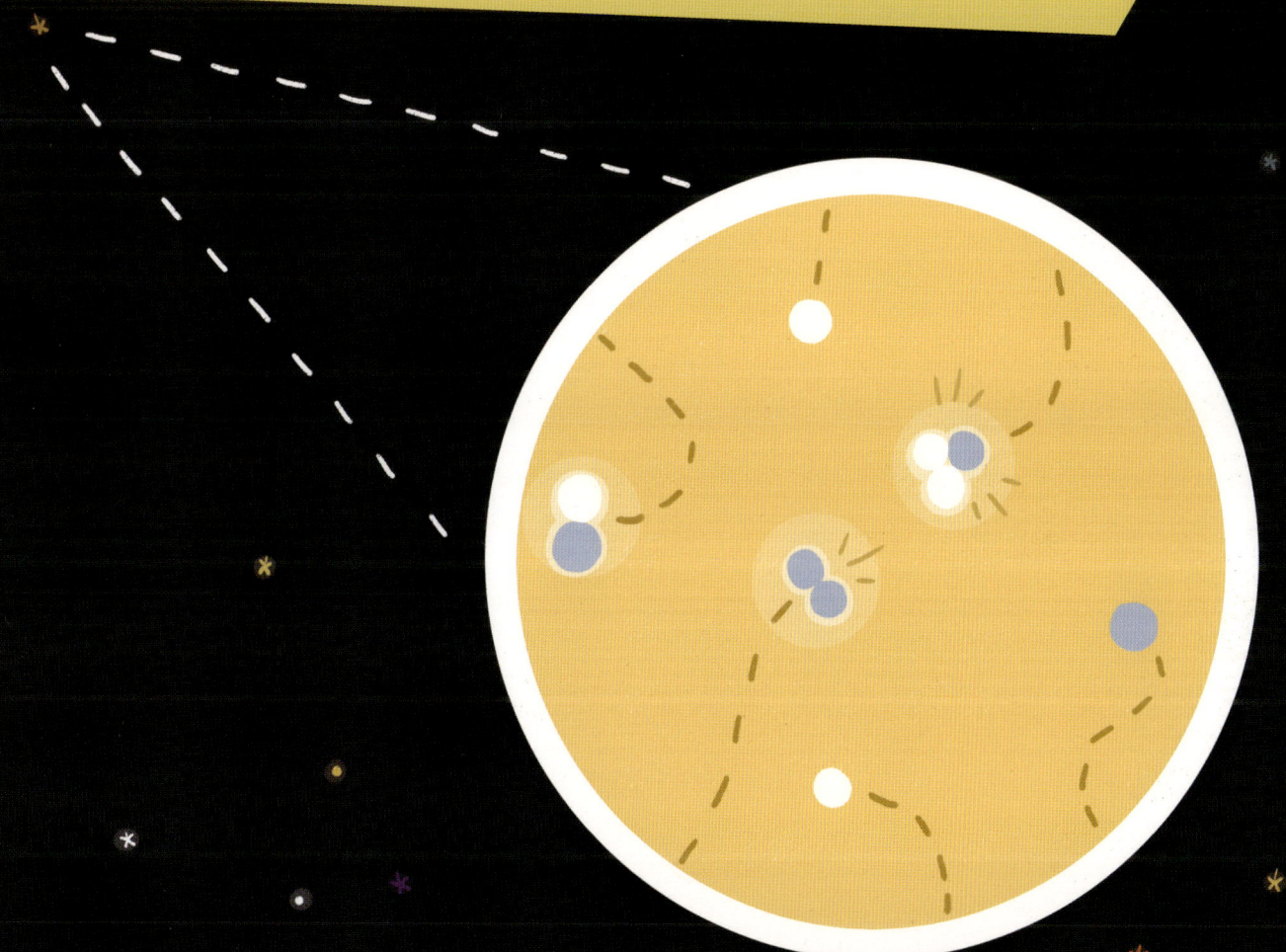

Sometimes, really old stars

EXPLODE!

The bits inside them whizz out into space like a giant starry sneeze.

The starry bits CRASH and CRUNCH together, making bigger and bigger space rocks.

The rocks spin and twirl, dancing around the stars.

Really **HUGE** space rocks are called planets.

One of these planets is our home, the world. We call it "Earth".

When God was first making Earth everything looked very different. All the crashing space rocks made it very, **VERY** hot!

So hot that the rock was all sticky and gloopy.

There was no air to breathe; no sea to swim in.

There were no trees to climb, and no animals at all.

Earth was just a big ball of **gooey** space rock. It took a long time to cool down.

As Earth got colder, the rocks around the outside got harder, making the ground we walk on. This is called Earth's "crust", because it's like a hard crust on a squishy loaf of bread.

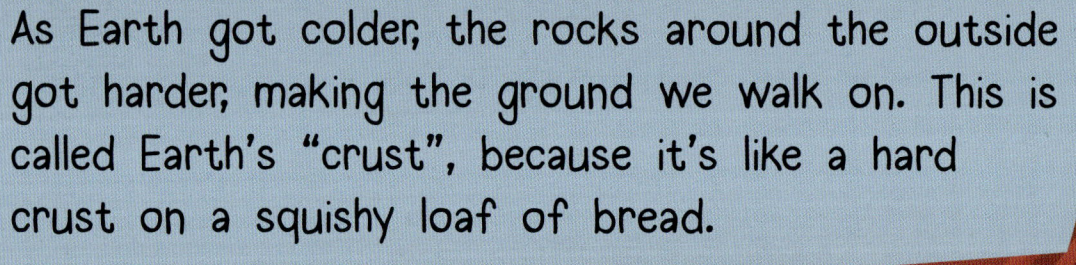

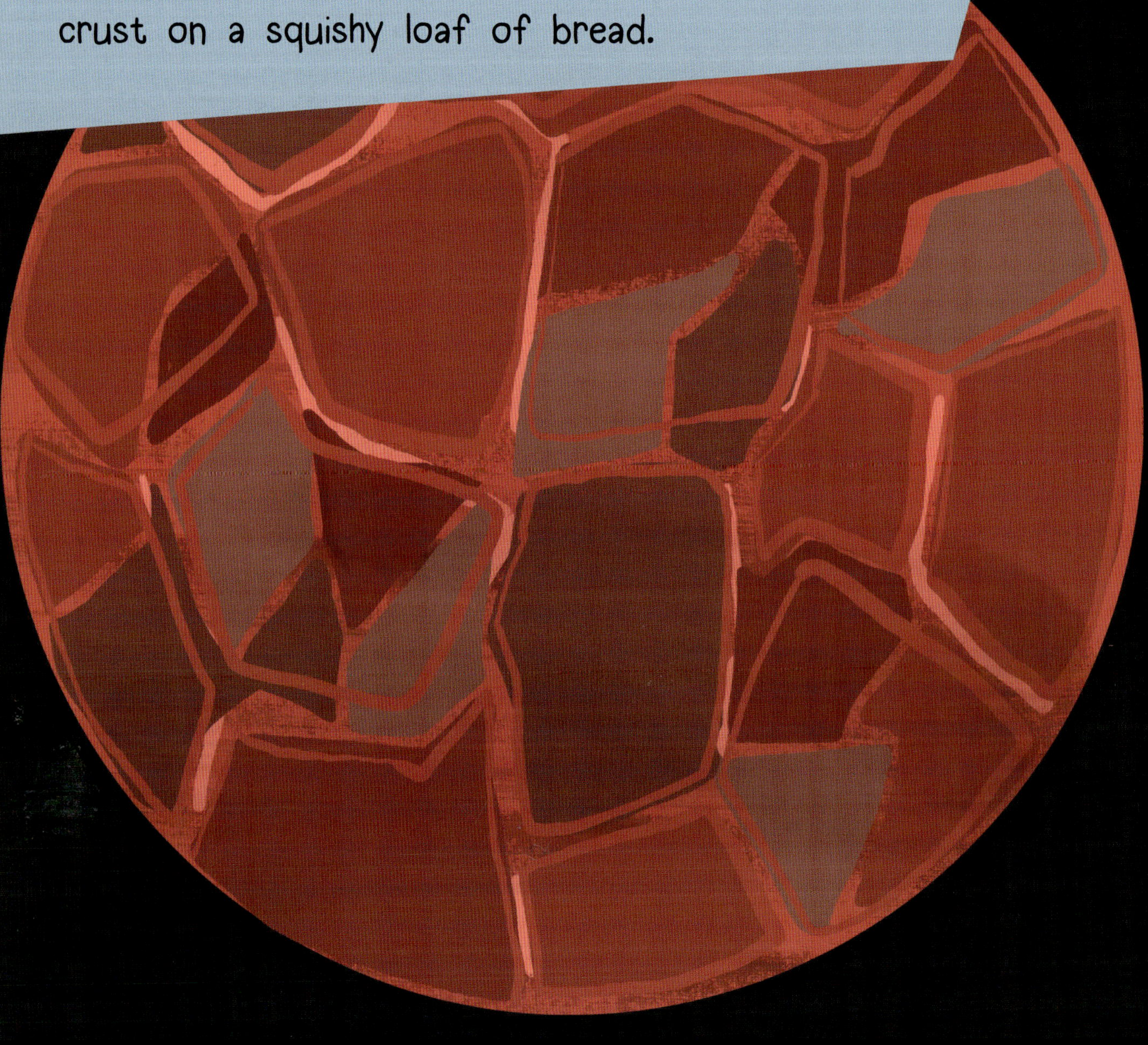

Under the hard crust the rock is still very **HOT**.

In special places, it gets very melty and bubbles up through the crust. We call these "volcanoes".

Volcanoes can also shoot up boiling water like huge kettles! The water makes **BIG** rain clouds.

Rain from these clouds might be how God made Earth's very first seas.

Clouds aren't only made by volcanoes. Every day, water from puddles, lakes, and seas gets warmed by the Sun and floats up into the sky to make clouds.

Clouds can be HUGE and FLUFFY,

small and wispy,

white,

grey,

or black
and stormy.

They can float a long way
before they drop rain into garden
puddles and steamy rainforests,
or even snow at the North Pole!

When God was first making Earth, water helped new living things to grow. They grew in the brand new seas and then all over the land.

Now, from pretty garden flowers to snowy mountain trees and spiky desert cacti, water helps plants grow almost

EVERYWHERE!

God's **AMAZING** Earth filled up with animals too!

Elephants and emus, monkeys and manatees, lobsters and lizards... from the highest mountains to the deepest seas, animals live everywhere!

God is so clever and creative!

Seas, volcanoes, plants, animals, and even people – everything on Earth comes from those tiny particles squashed together inside stars!

God loves it when we explore, learn about, and take care of His Earth.

People have invented things like microscopes, medicine, and recycling to help us find out about the world and look after it.

Maybe one day you'll discover something new about God's wonderful Earth?

God has made an amazing world, and He loves everything He has made.

EXPERIMENTS AND ACTIVITIES

Why not try out these fun activities to help your little ones think a bit more about the amazing world God has made? You can find some helpful hints and tips at www.faradaykids.com/activities.

CHOCOLATE 'EARTH'S CRUST'

Help your little ones think about the amazing properties of God's world by seeing what happens when you heat and cool chocolate. Watch it become "melty" and "gloopy" and then set hard like Earth's hard crust (this is especially yummy if you watch it set on ice cream, or around gooey truffle "earths"!)

VOLCANO EXPLOSION!

Wonder at the power of God's amazing creation with a homemade volcano! Simple kitchen ingredients can be combined to create all sorts of explosive fun. There are so many ways to play with this activity, so enjoy experimenting!

CLOUD CRAFTS

Get creative with fun shaving foam paintings and think about God's creativity in making all the different kinds of clouds. Why not see how many you can spot in the sky on different days?

LEAF TREASURE HUNT

Enjoy the wonderful variety in God's amazing creation as you and your little ones search out different kinds of plants, trees, and other living things. Use a guide to help you identify them, or even collect some fallen leaves to take home or use in craft projects.

CRESS HEADS

Explore how God's plants really can grow almost anywhere as you create these fun, "hairy" characters, which will help your little ones learn how plants need light and water to grow.

A NOTE ABOUT SCIENCE AND THE BIBLE

As humans, we love to question, explore, and discover the world around us, and our place in it. *God Made the World* is written to help even the youngest humans begin to explore the world God made them to be a part of.

God Made the World gives an inviting overview of mainstream scientific ideas about how the world works. It celebrates the glimpse that science offers into God as creator, and the way our wonder can increase as we find out more about His universe.

Almost every book of the Bible talks about God as creator and His relationship with creation. The more we understand about who wrote each part of the Bible – when, why, and for whom – the more we can enjoy what they tell us about God.

The Bible doesn't discuss every part of God's creation. Dinosaurs, general relativity, black holes, bacteria, pandas or penguins don't get a look in! But this doesn't mean the Bible is inaccurate or outdated. Rather than talking about atomic structure or the speed of light thousands of years before people were asking questions about them, God led the authors to focus on His power, love, and authority in ways that were relevant and radical at the time, and still are today.

The Bible is full of people marvelling at the expanse of the stars, the beauty of God's creatures, and the processes of nature – seeing God's glory in it all.

> **"The heavens declare the glory of God"** *(Psalm 19:1)*
>
> **"Great are the works of the Lord, studied by all who delight in them."** *(Psalm 111:2)*

Today, all over the world, people are still drawn to worship God through exploring the expanse, depth, and intricacies of His creation. From the youngest child to the world's top scientists, God delights in our wonder at His creation.

> **"I believe God gave us intelligence so that we could investigate and appreciate the wonders of His creation."**
>
> Francis Collins
> *Geneticist*

> **"We are free to explore the universe with joyful curiosity, relying on God's faithfulness, discovering all the wonderful 'hows' and 'whens' of creation, about which scripture tells us 'who' and 'why.'"**
>
> Deborah Haarsma
> *Astrophysicist*

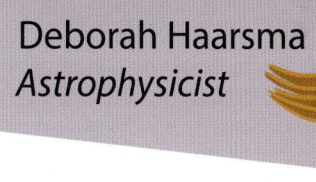

We hope that *God Made the World* will encourage you and your little ones to share in God's delight by exploring the creation He loves and experiencing wonder, awe, and worship for yourselves. To explore further, check out our other books or head to our website: www.faradaykids.com.